WELCOME
TO
ANTIQUE BOTANICALS IV
- AN ADULT COLORING BOOK -

ISBN: 1519738013
ISBN-13: 978-1519738011

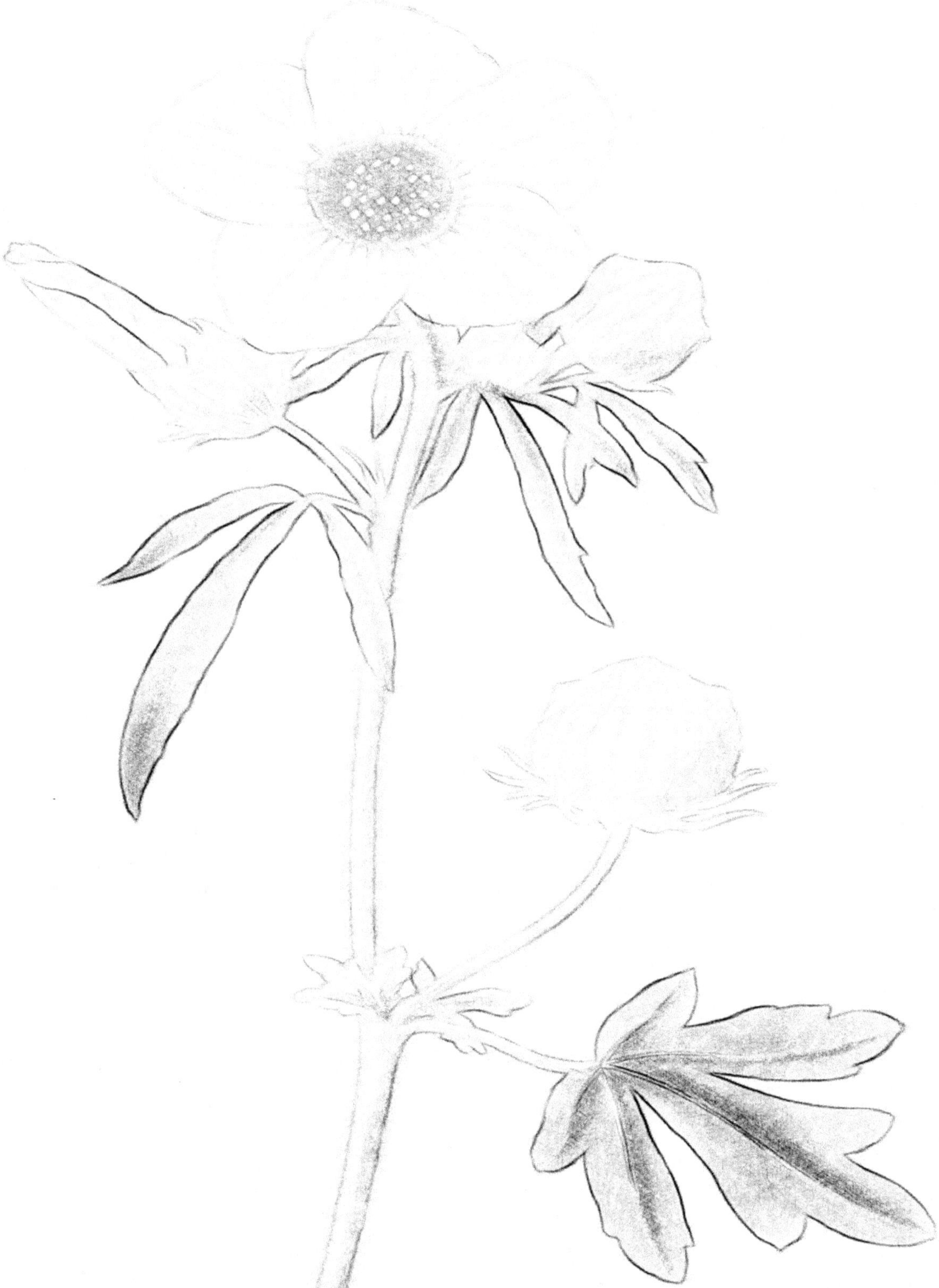

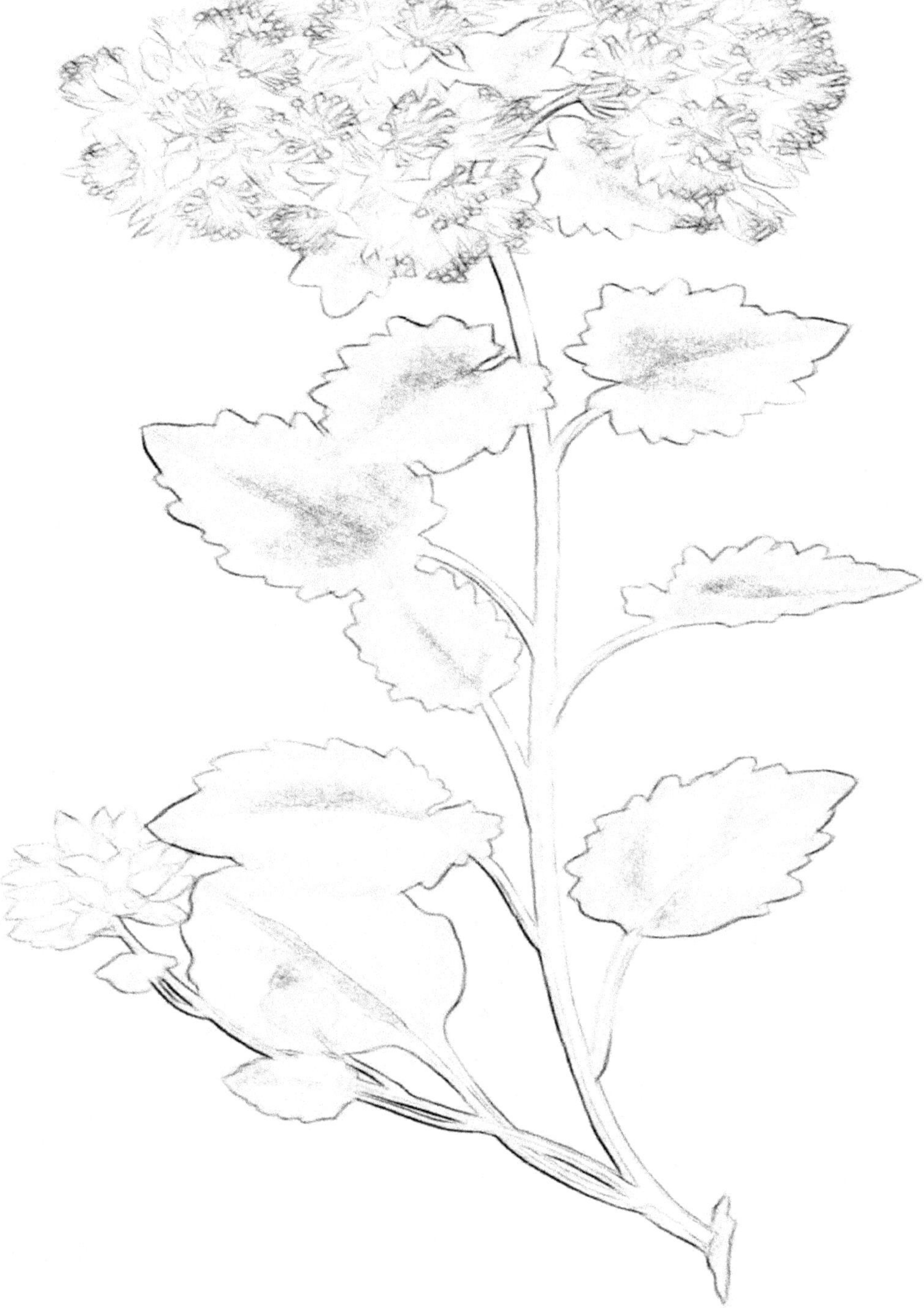

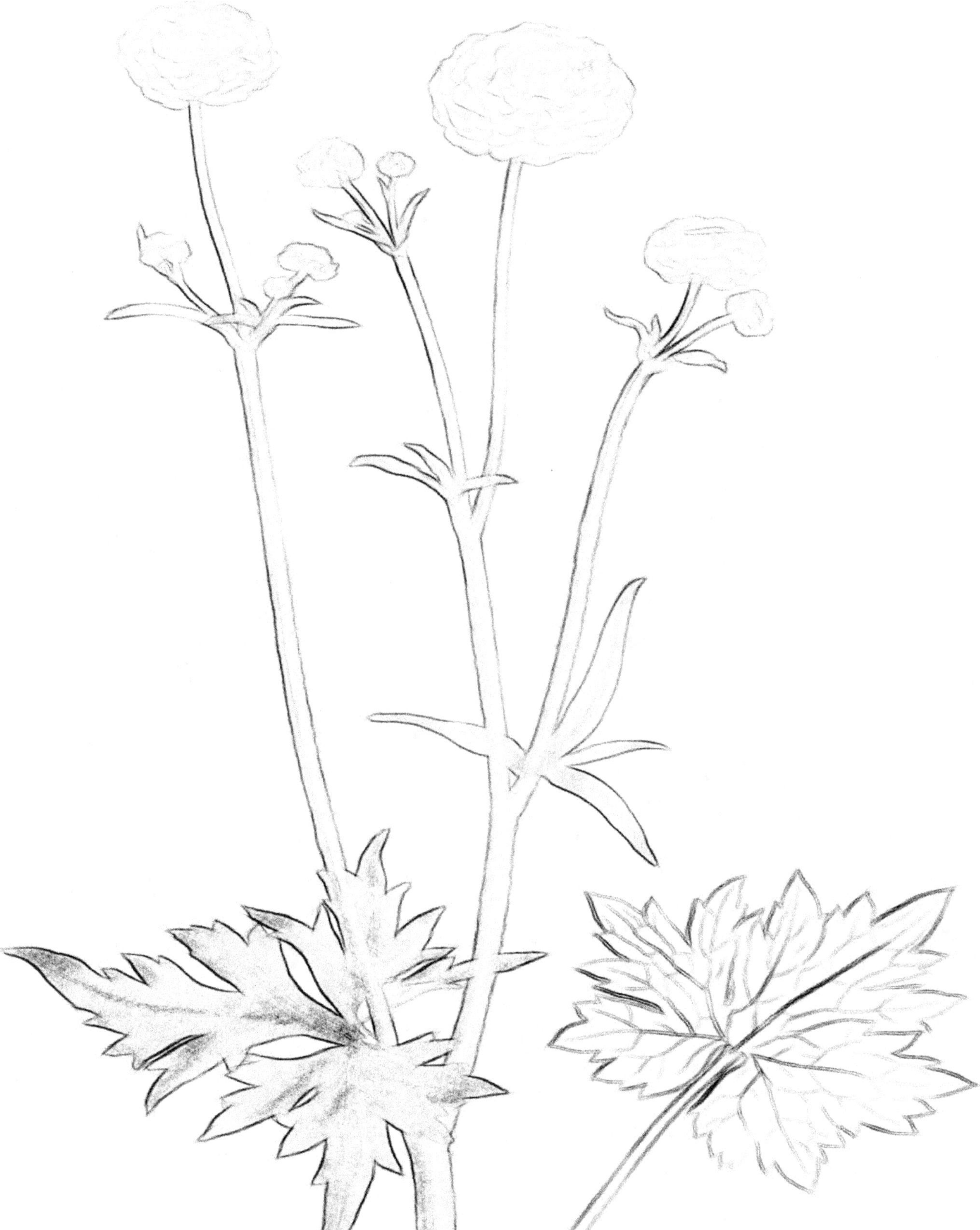

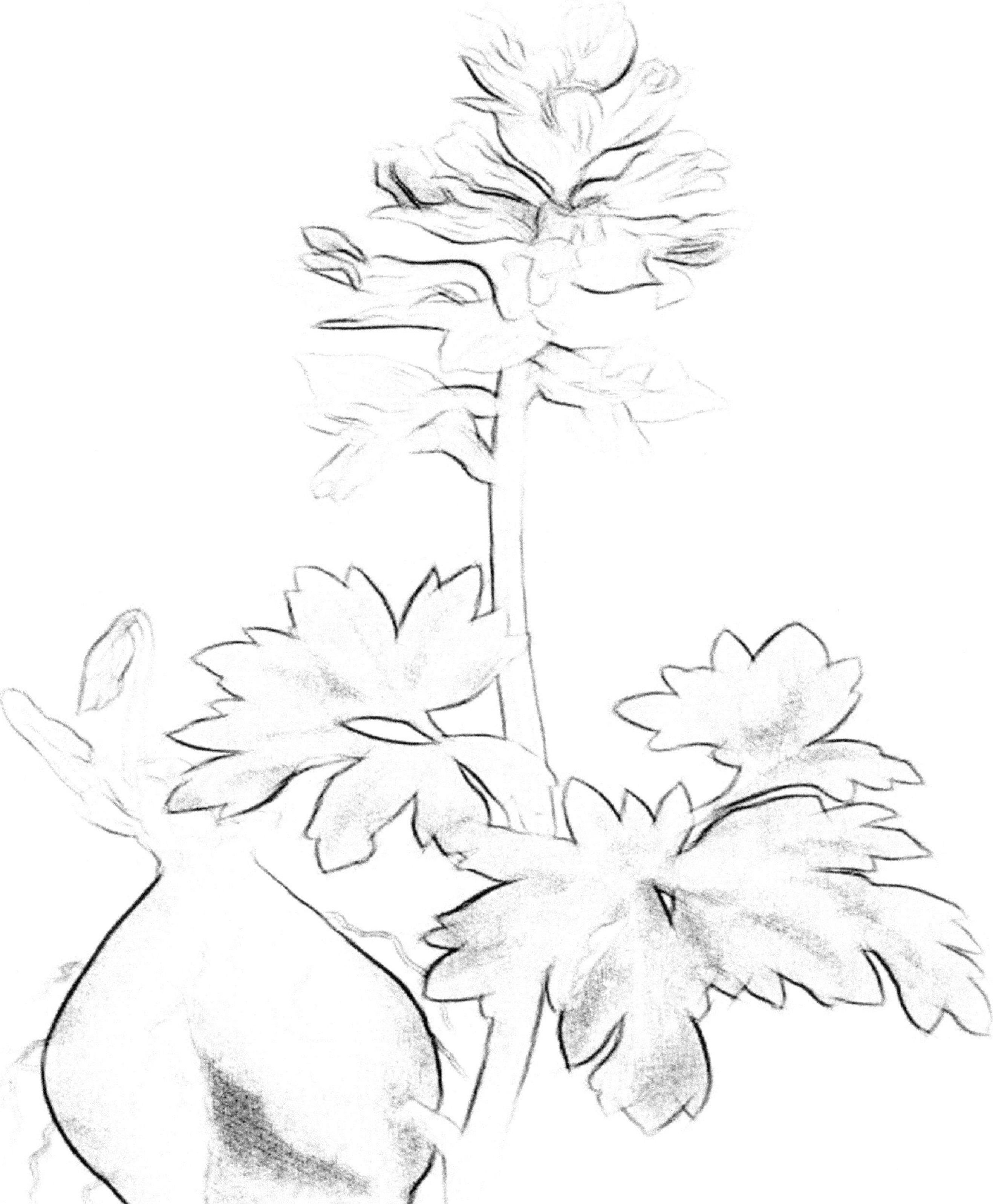

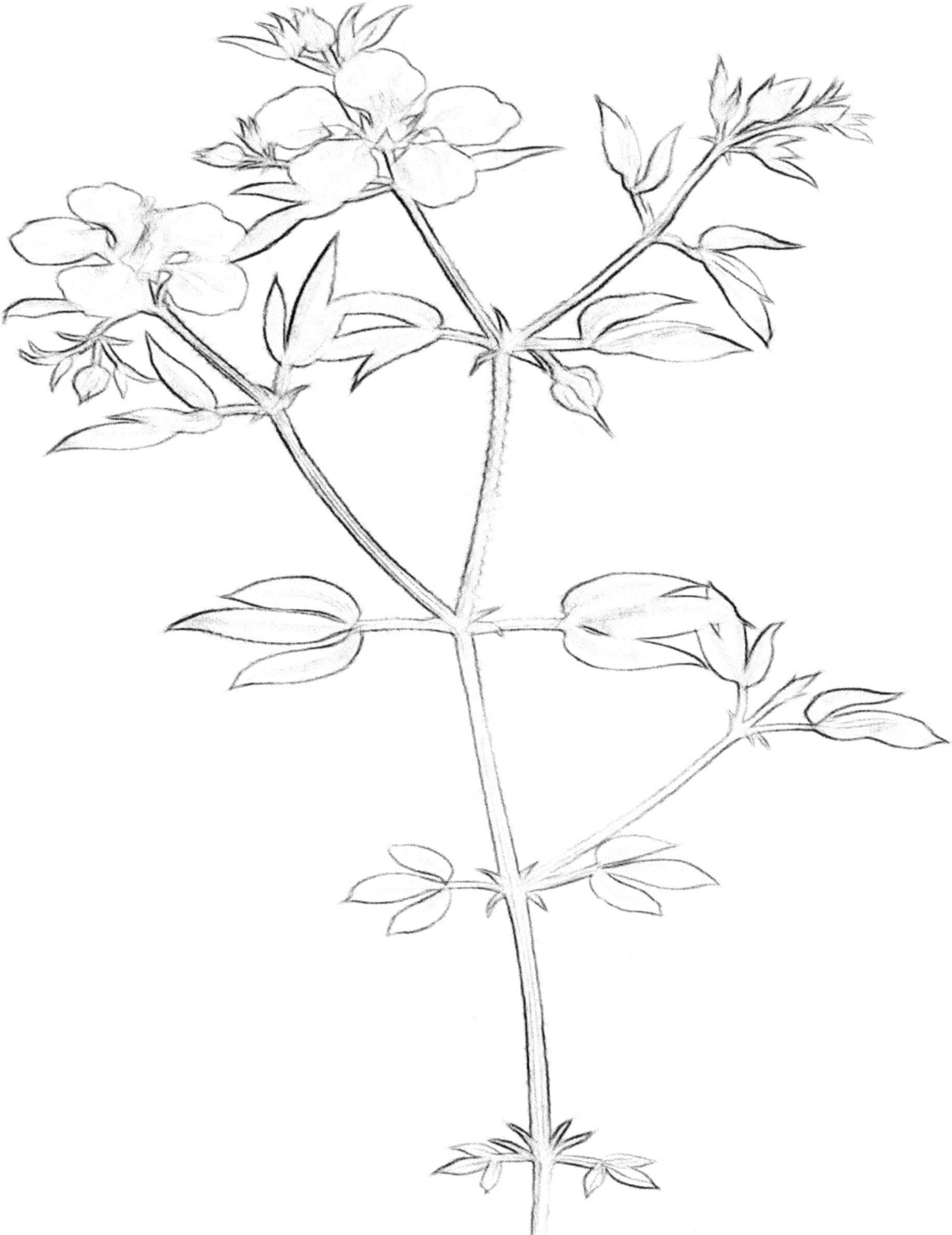

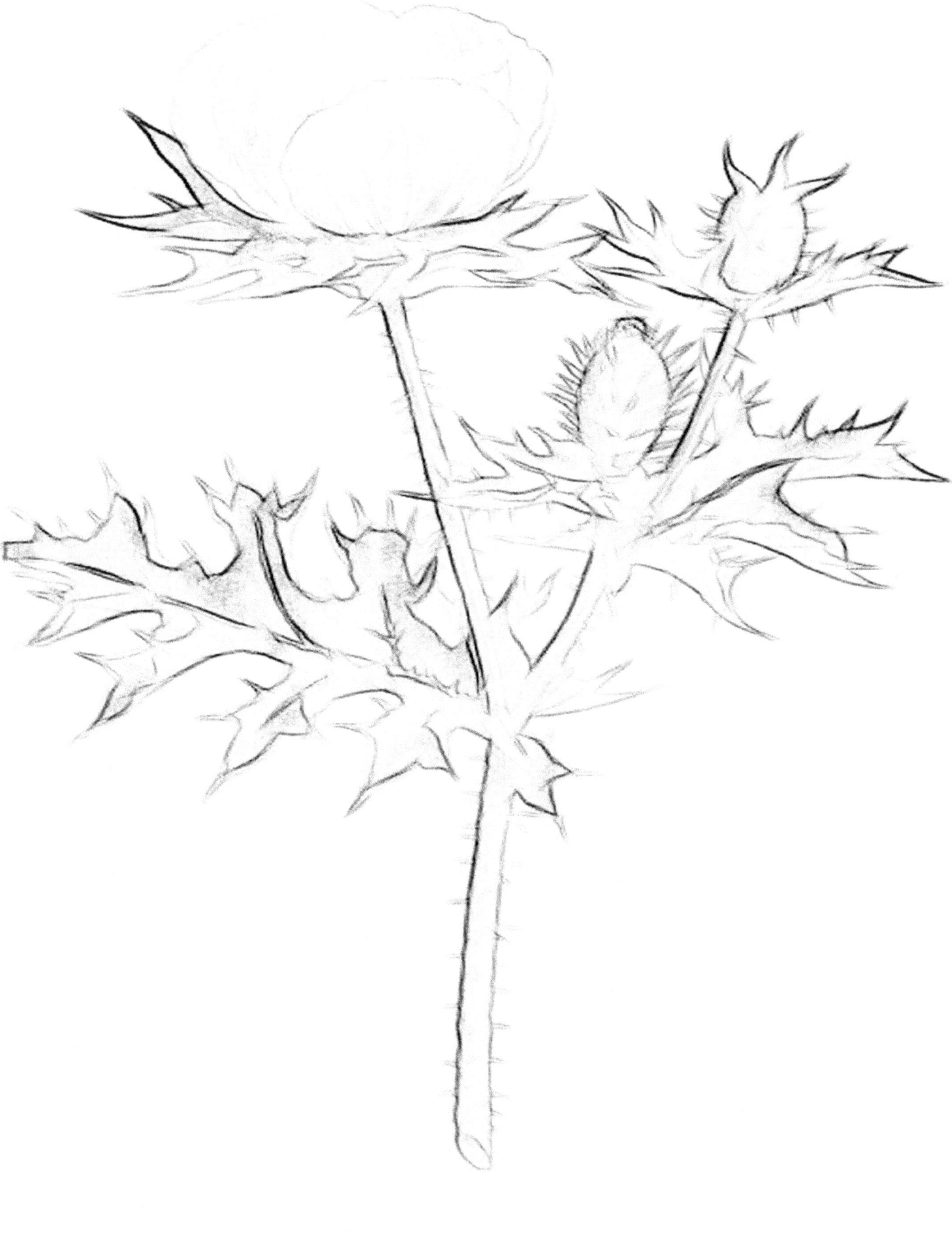

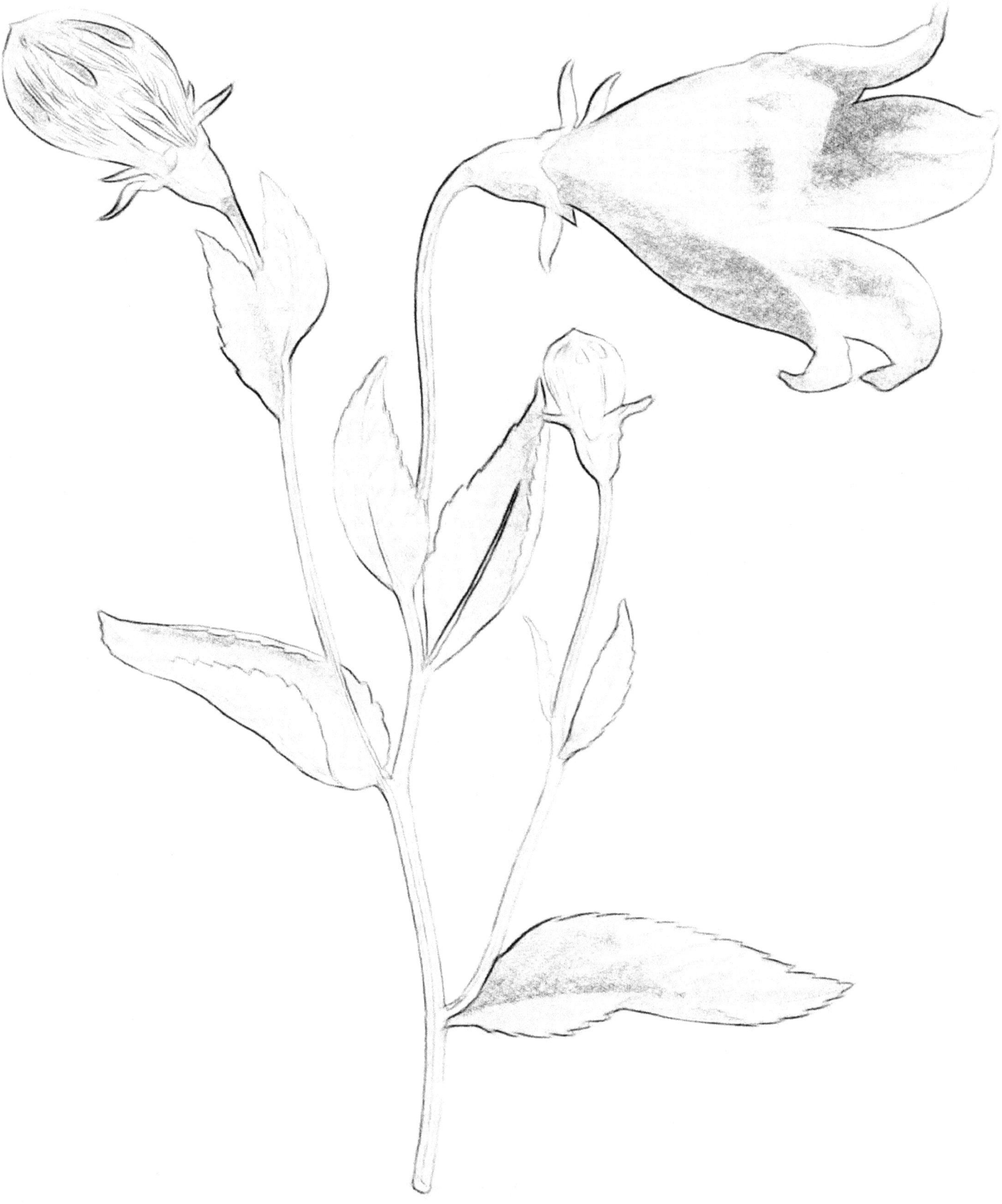

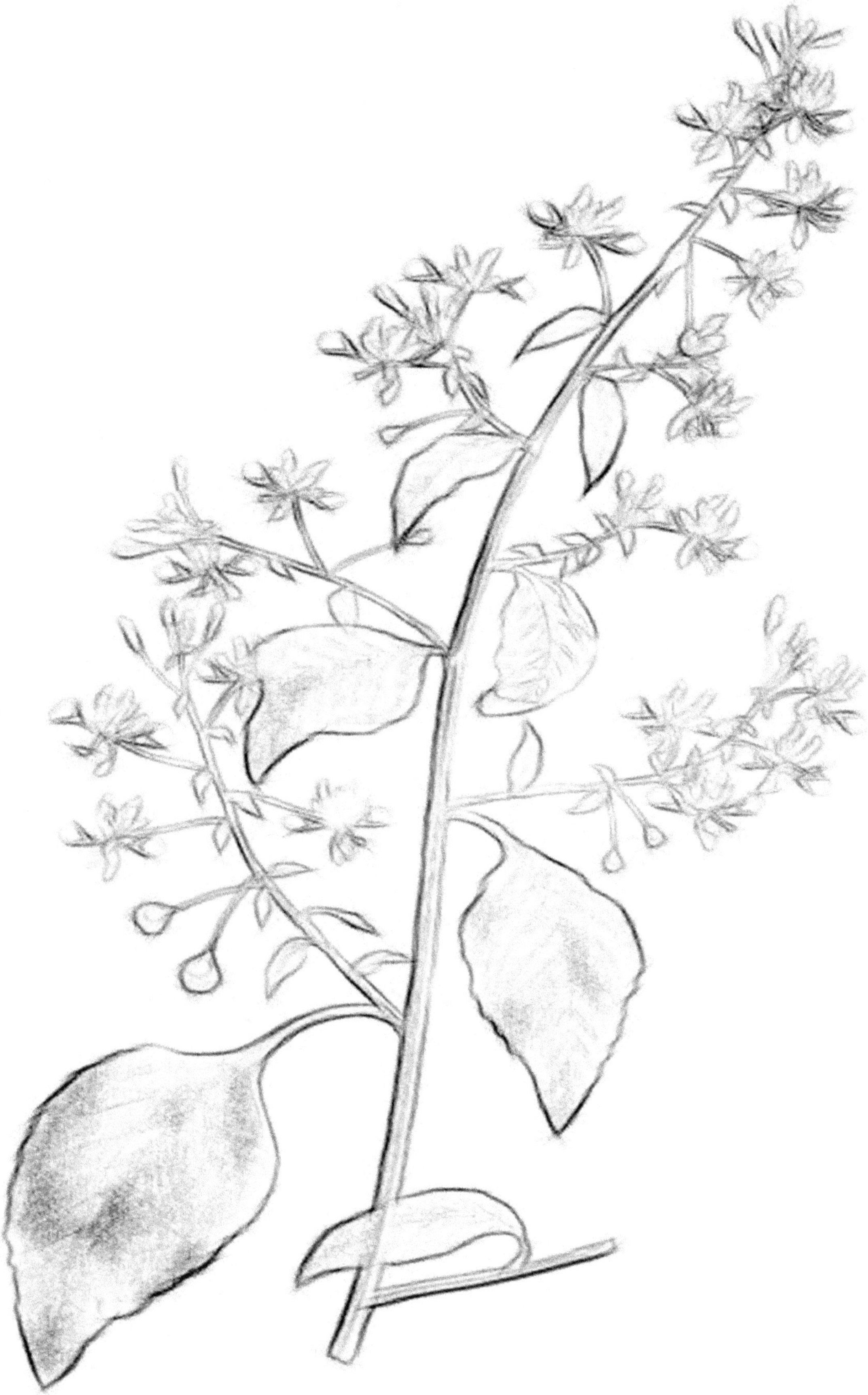

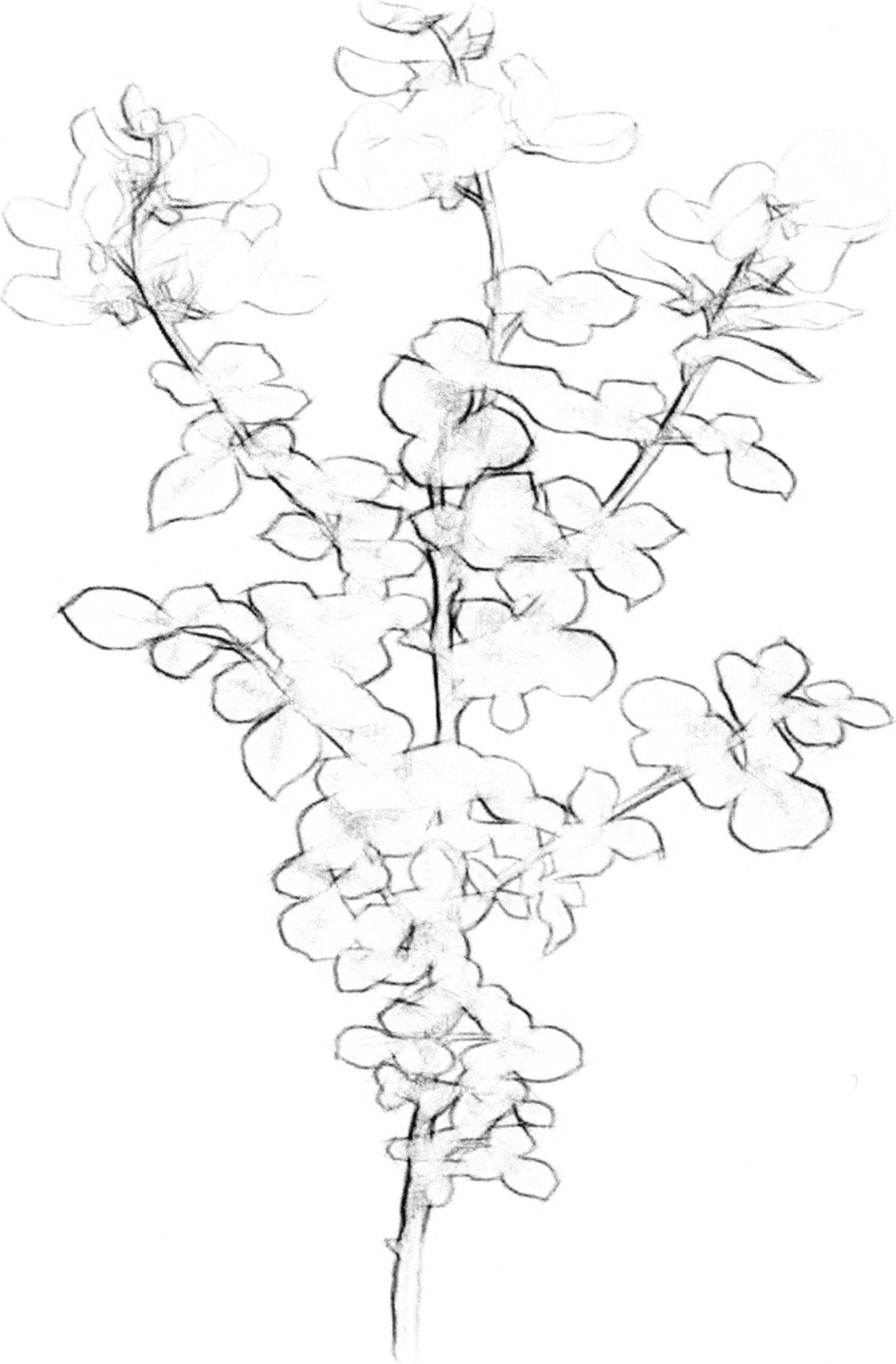

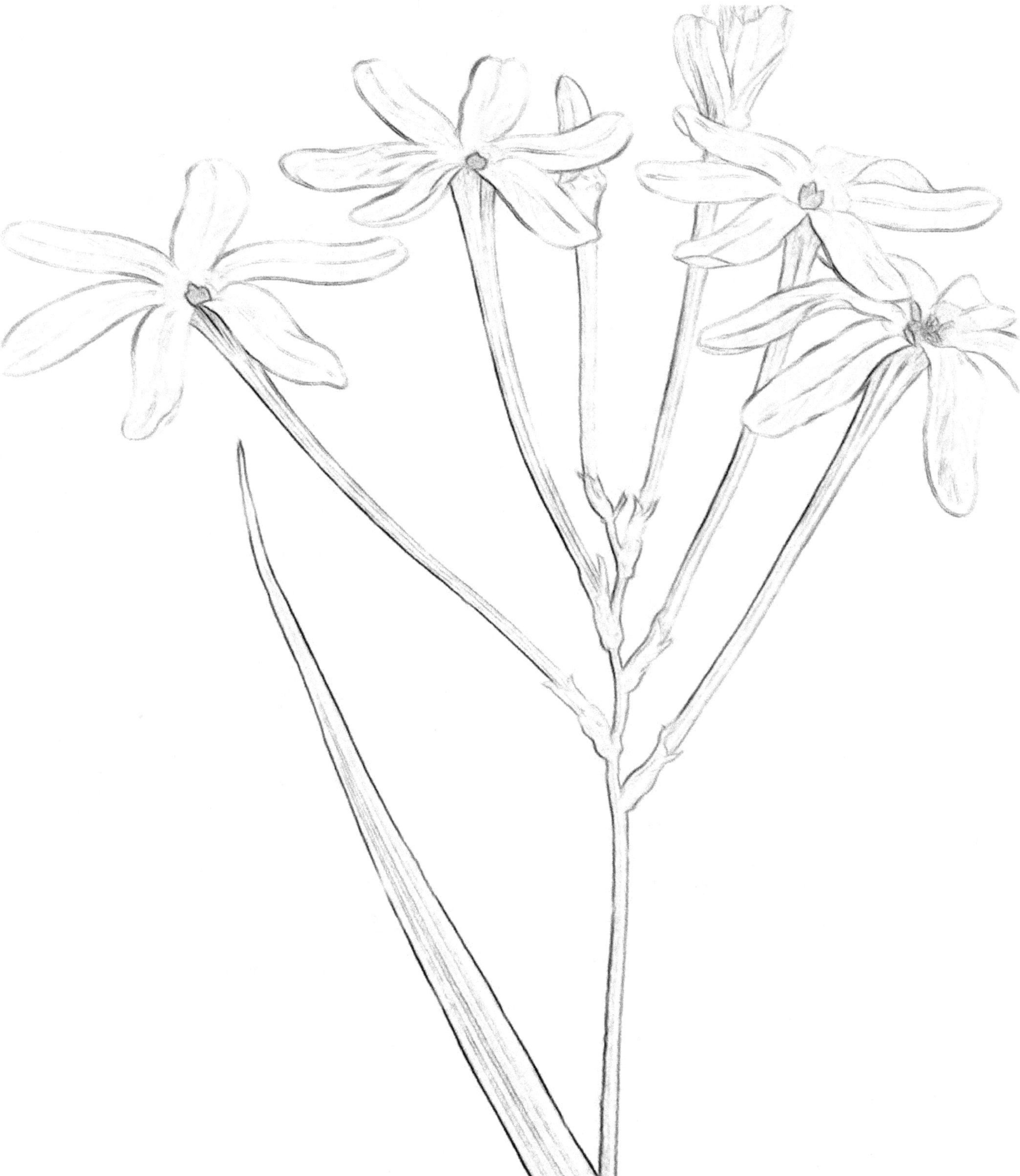

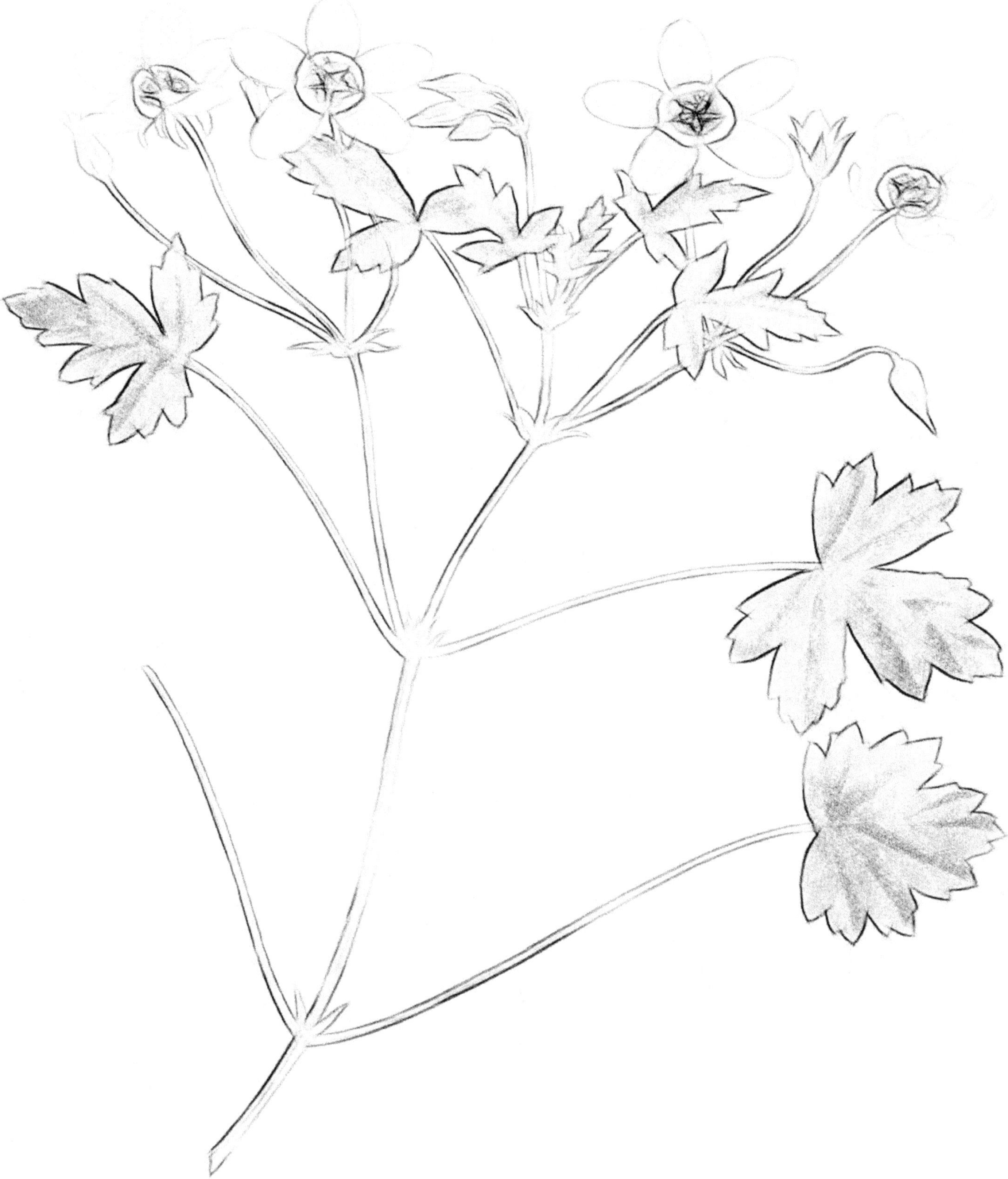

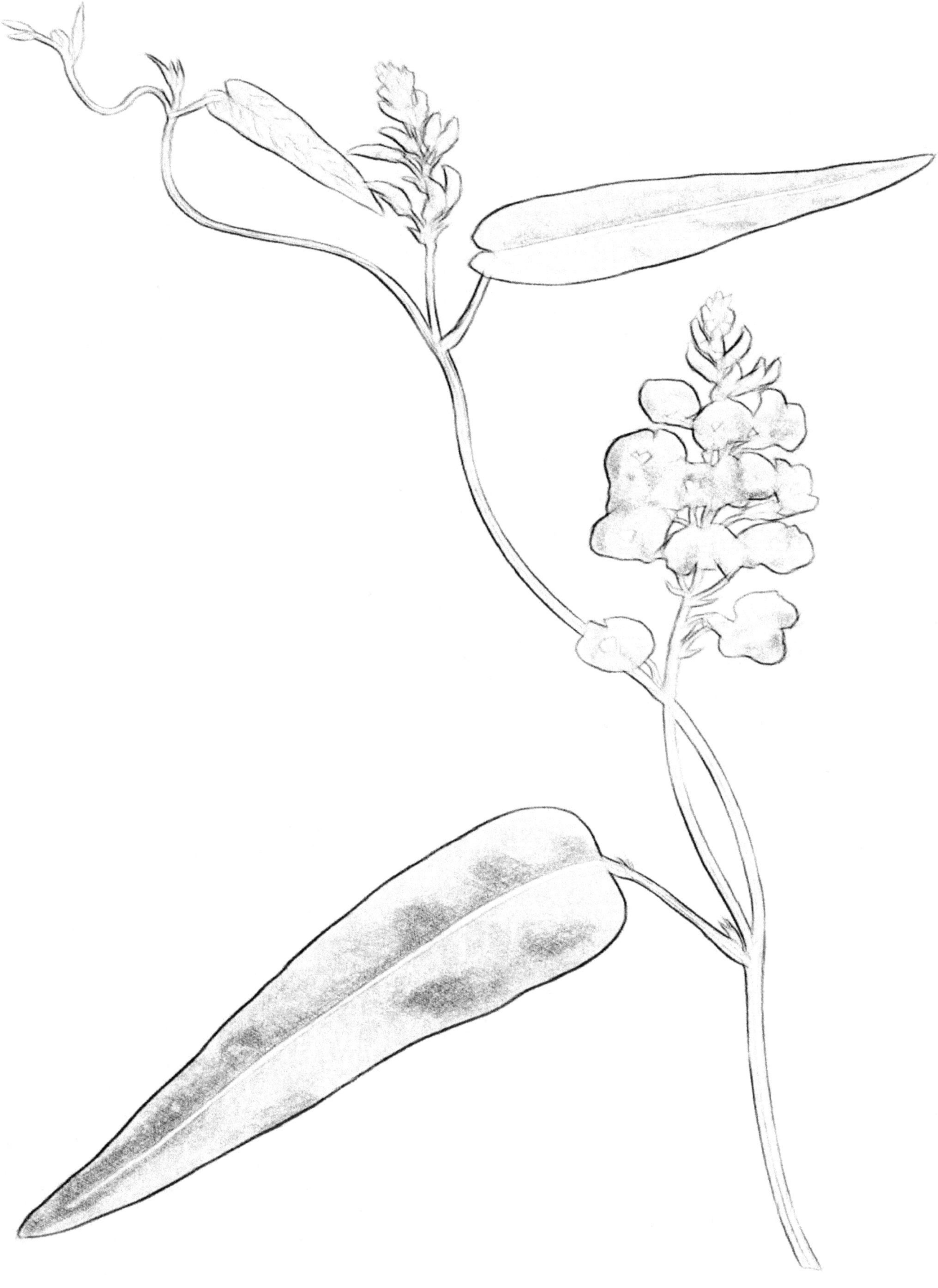

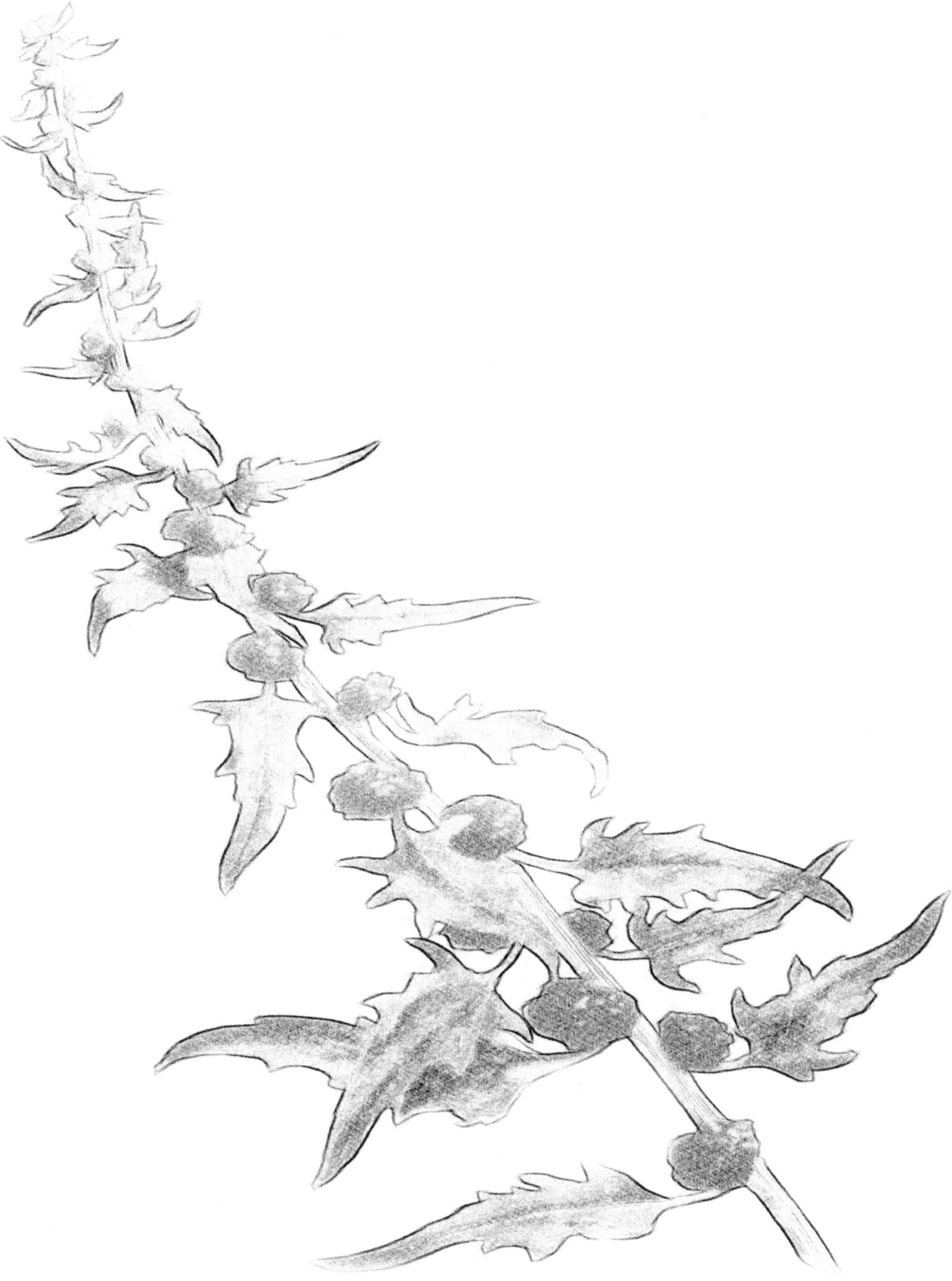

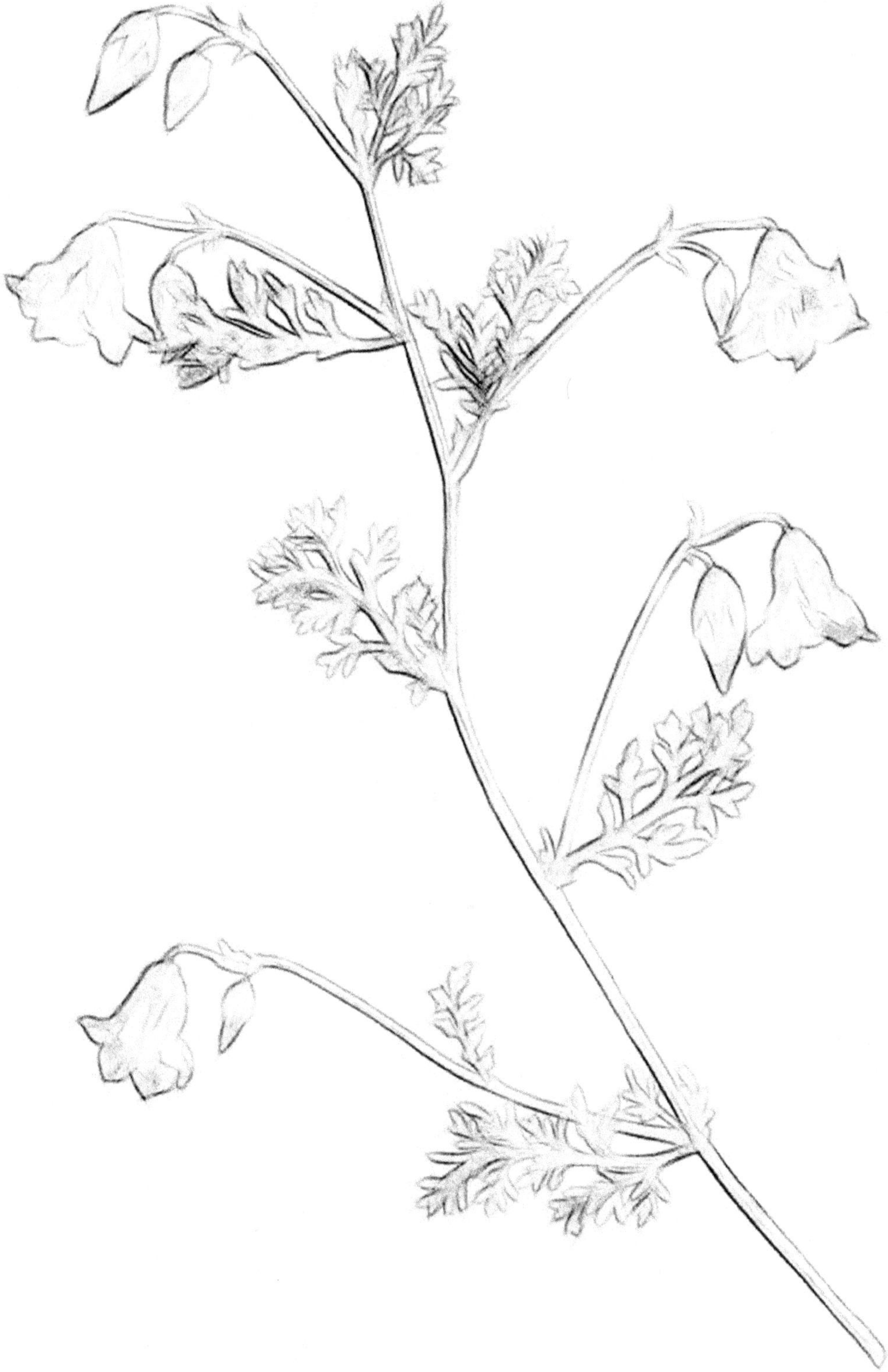

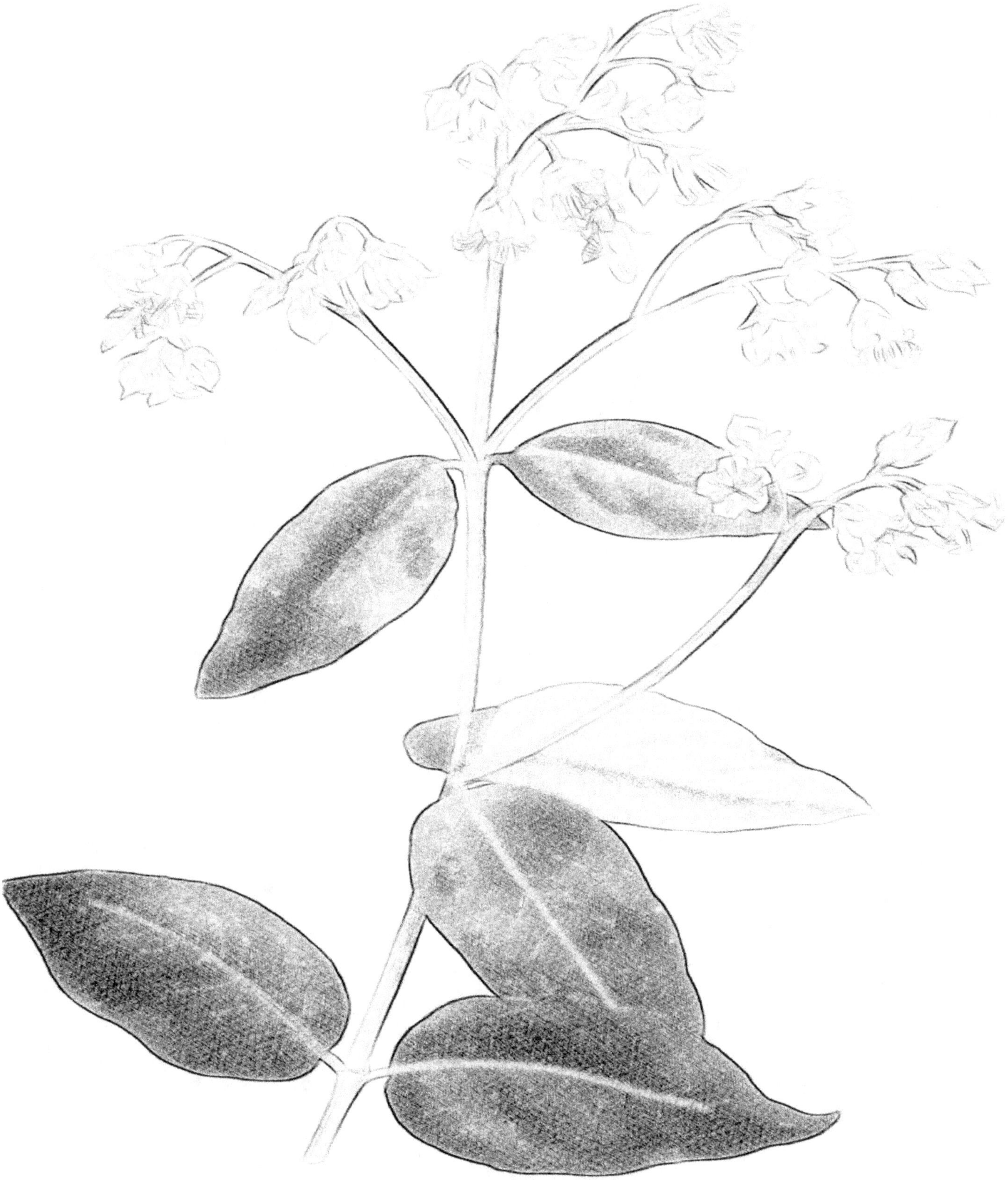

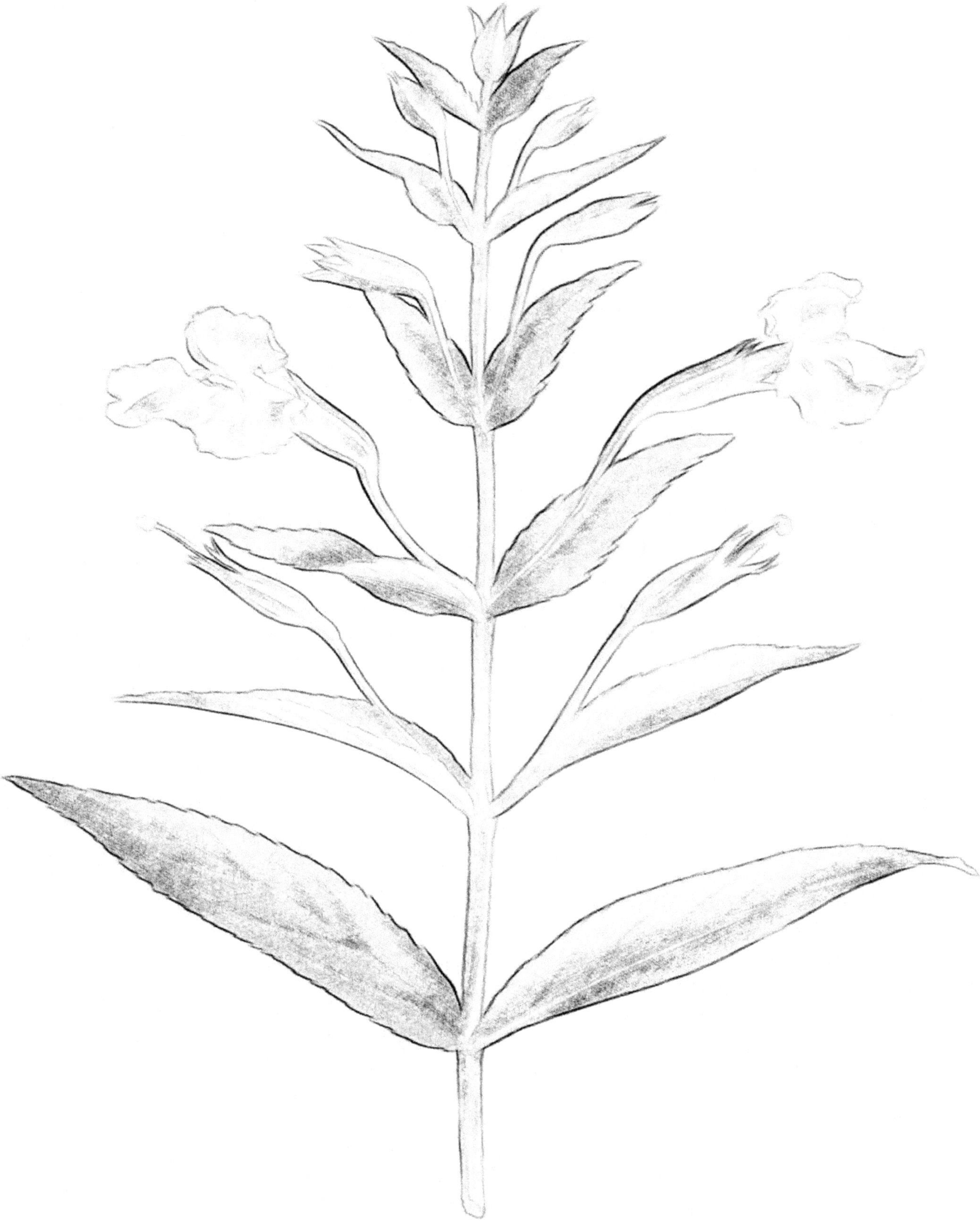

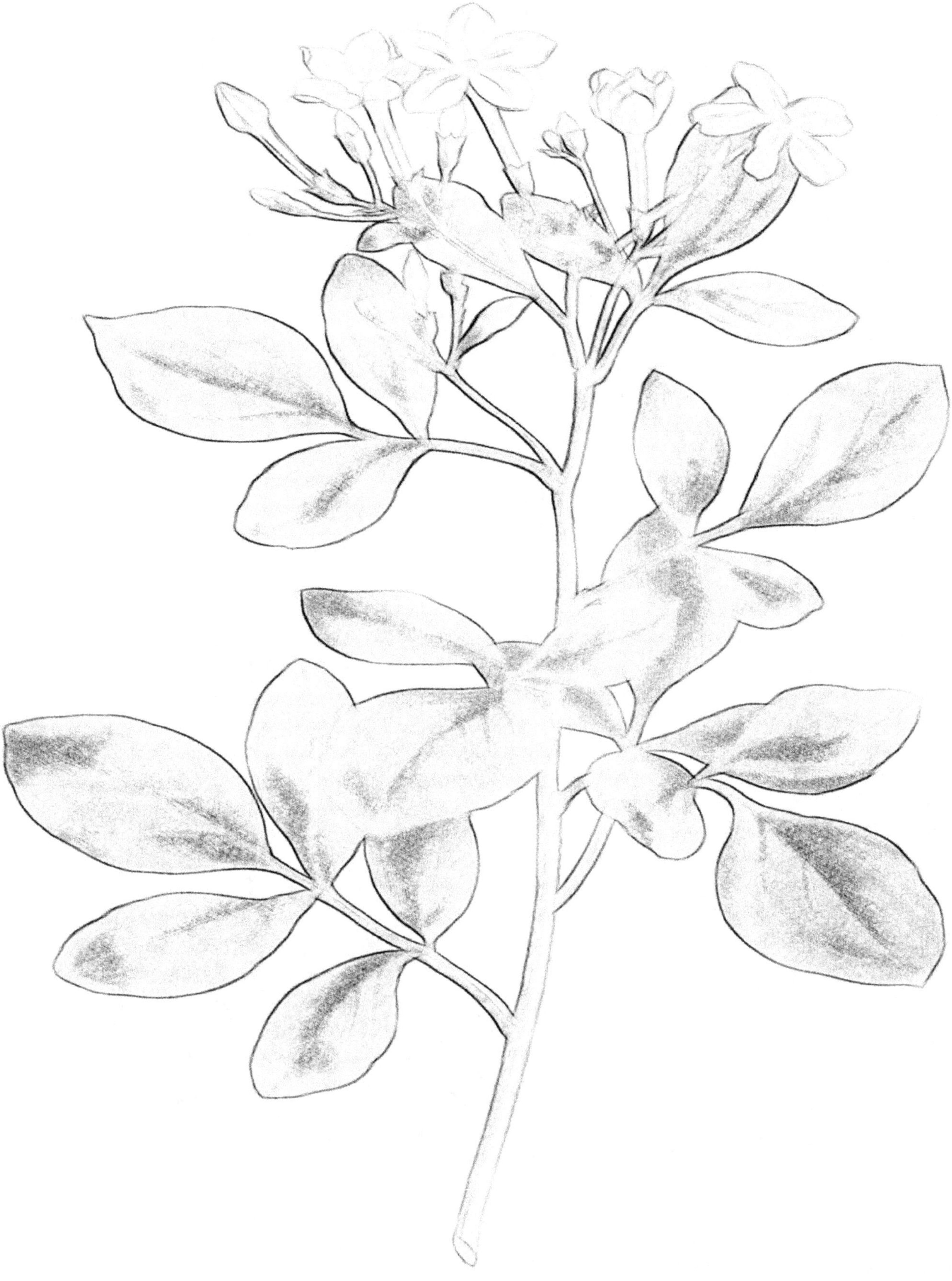

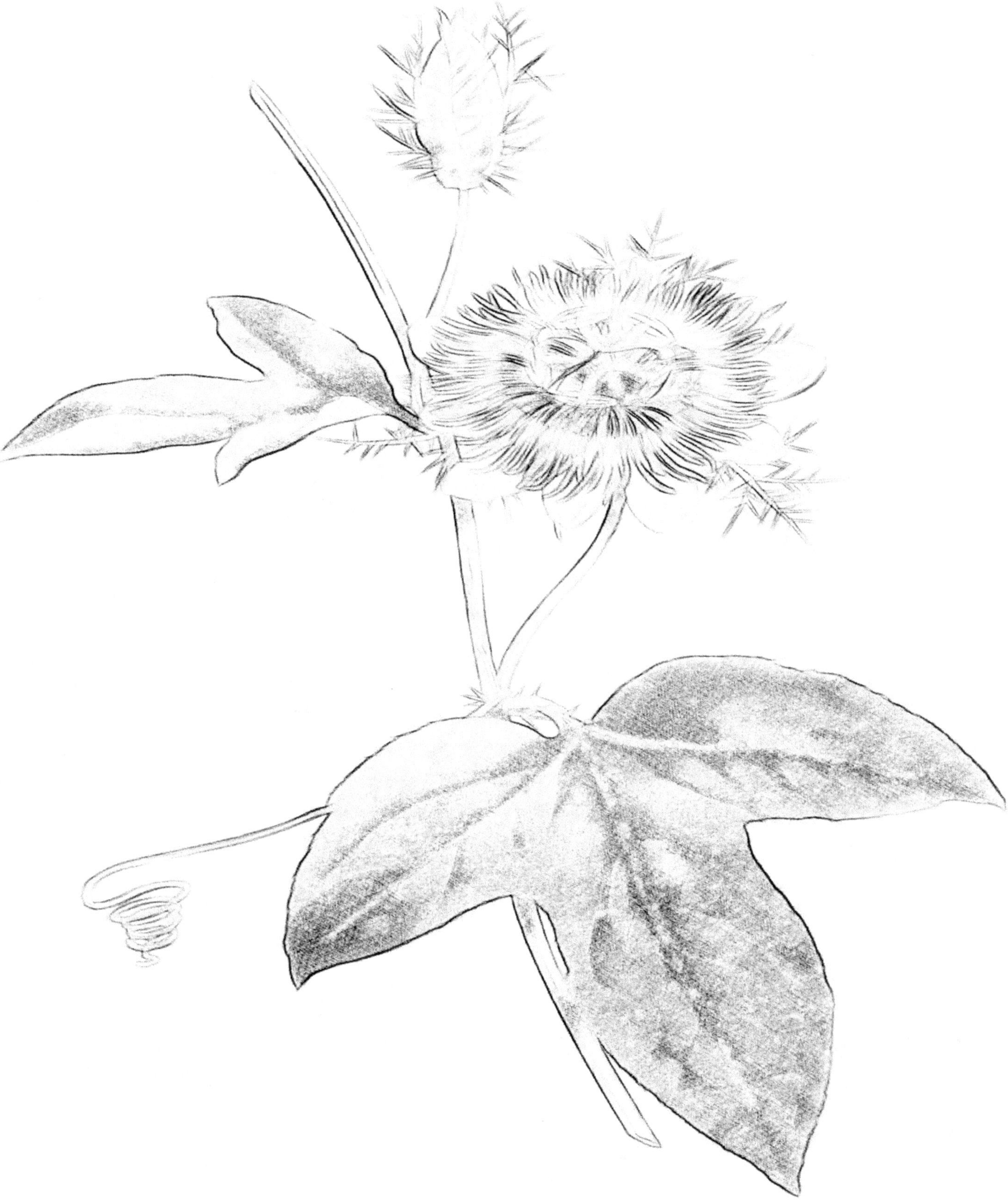

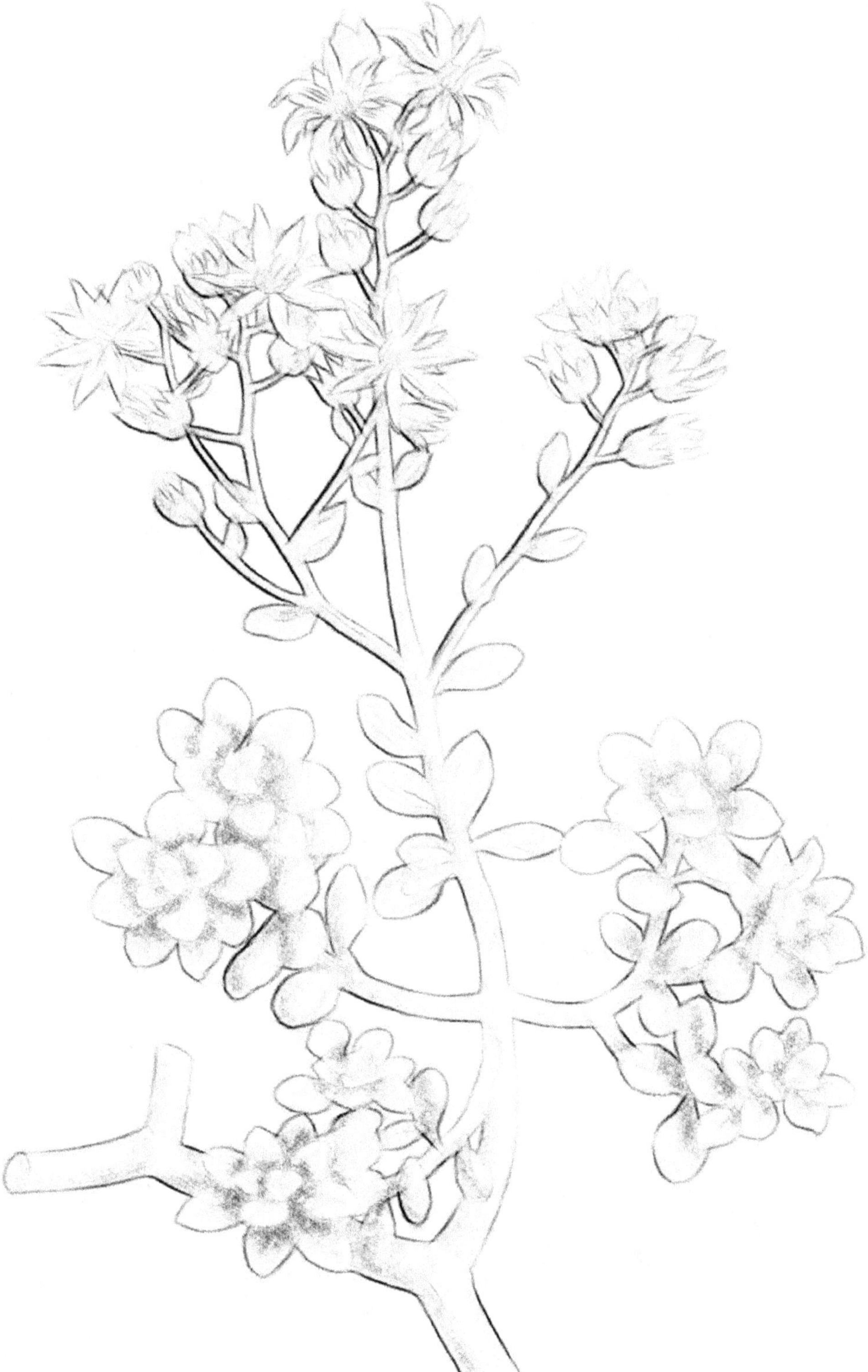

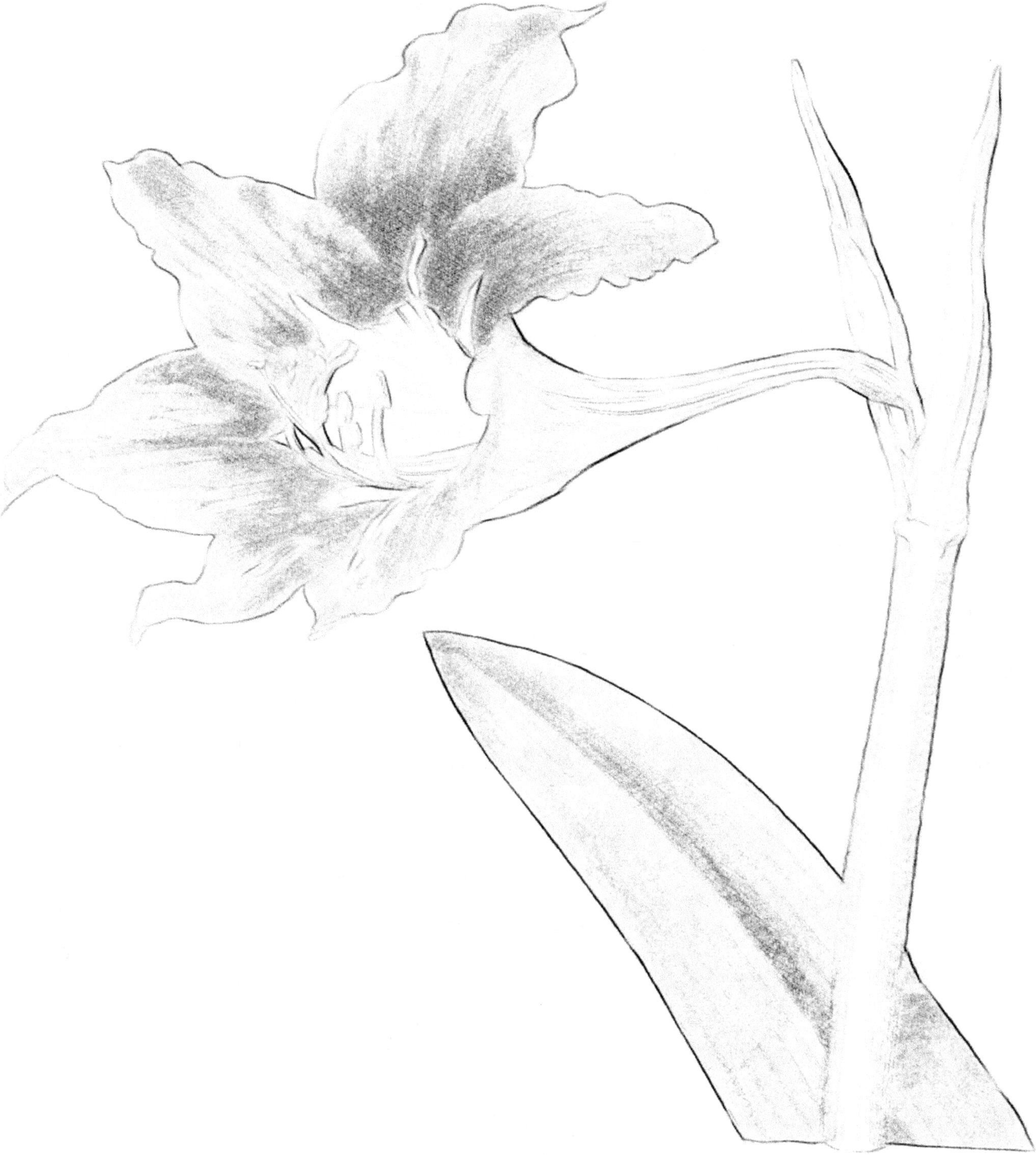

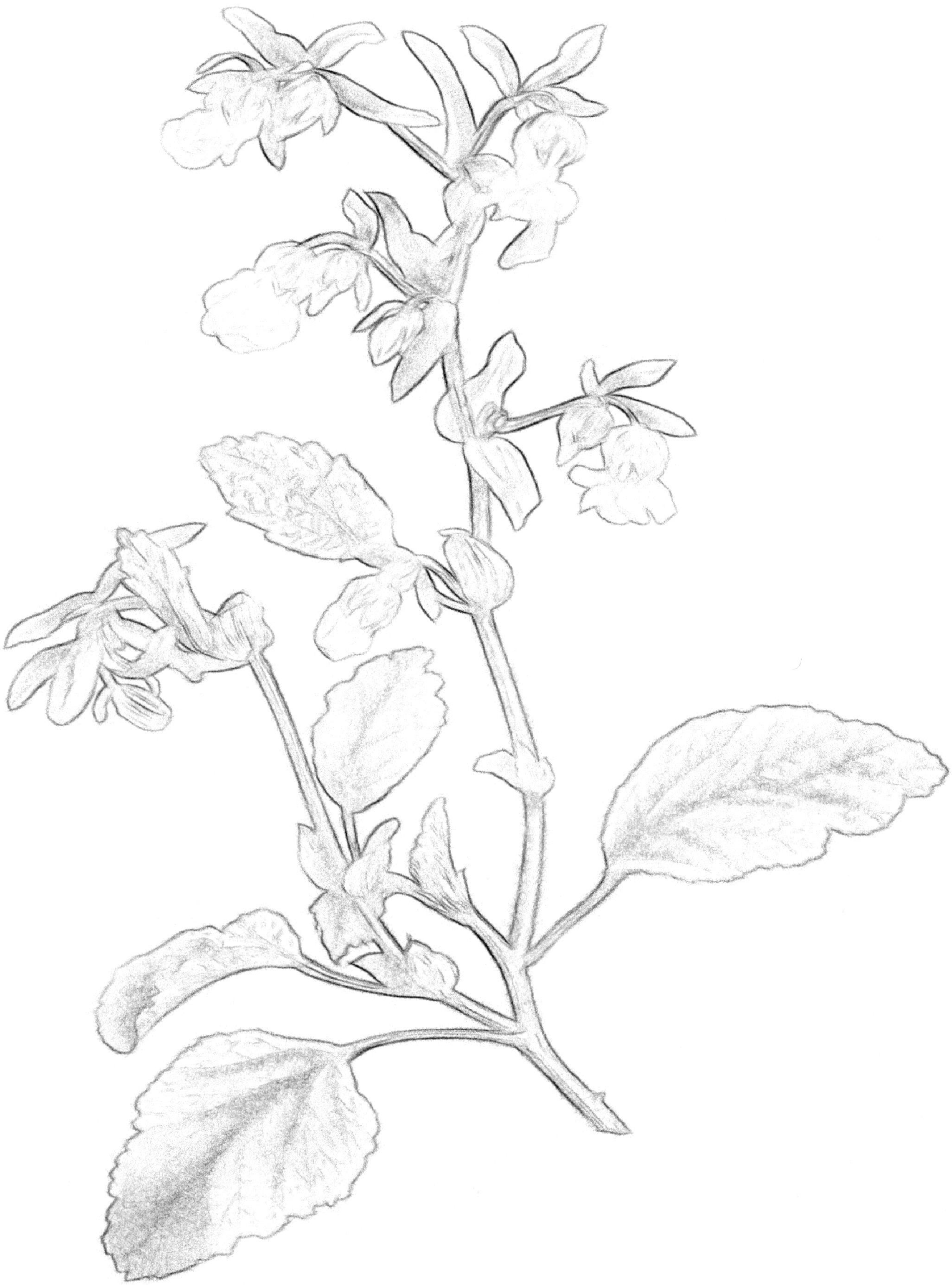

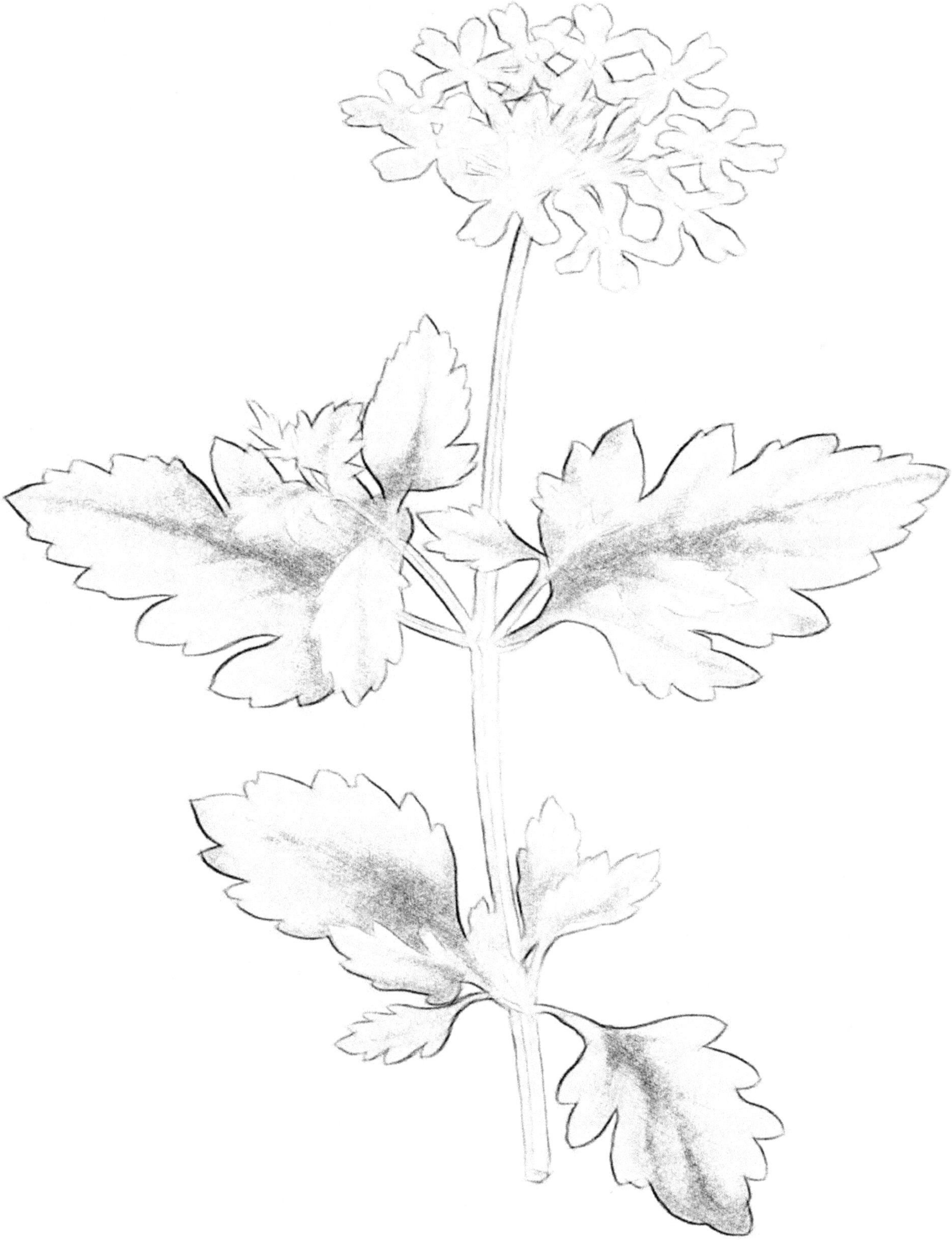

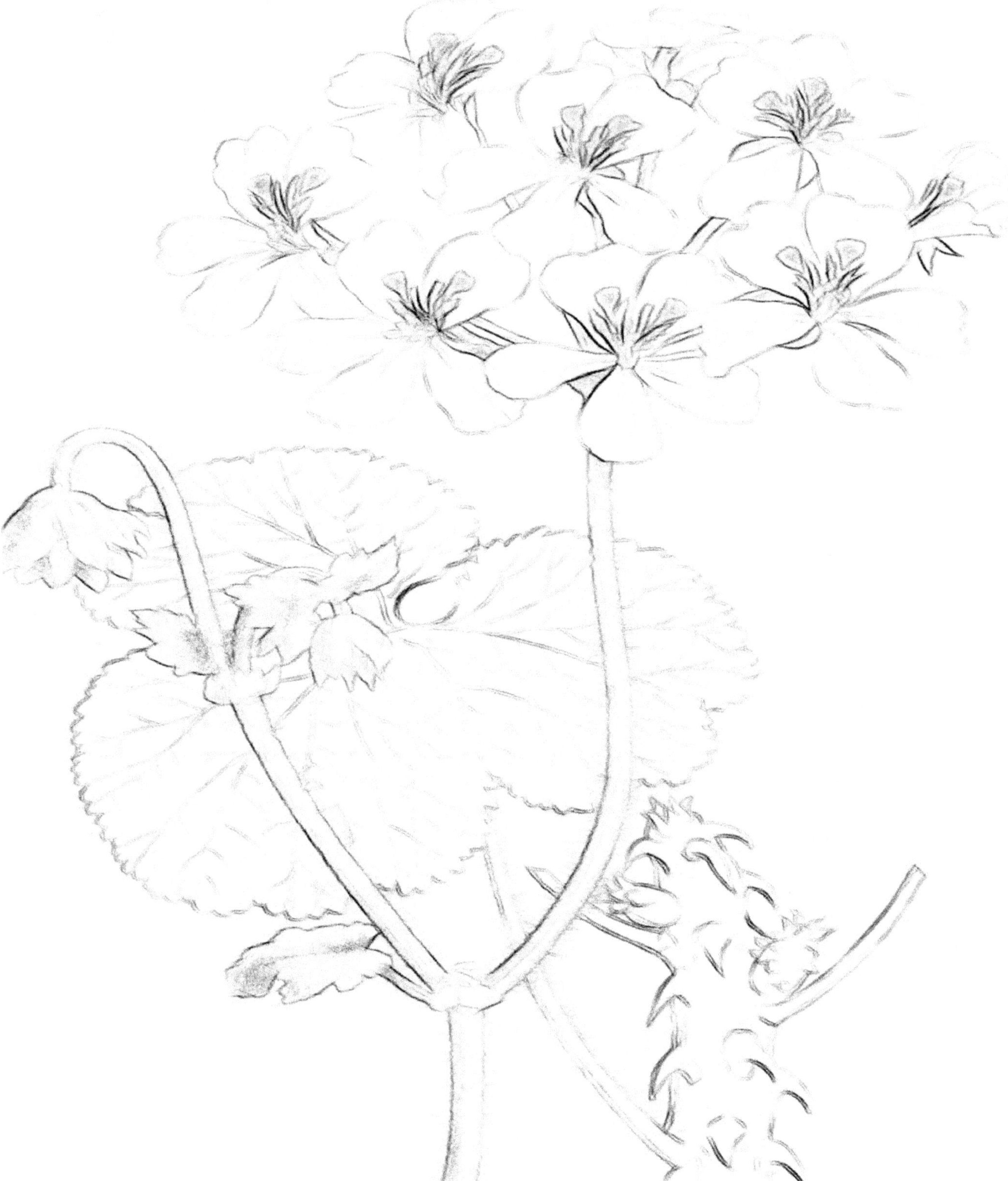

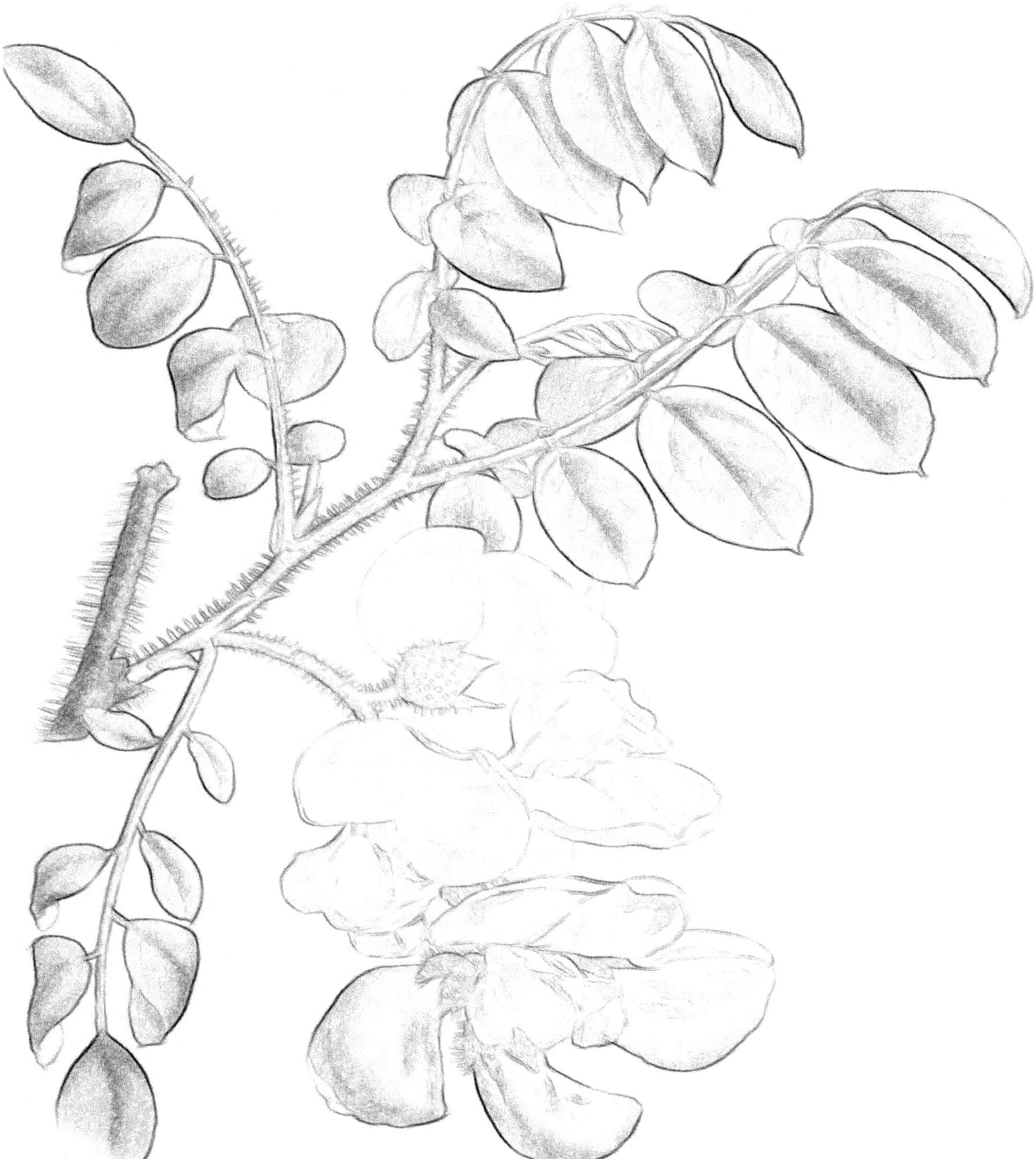

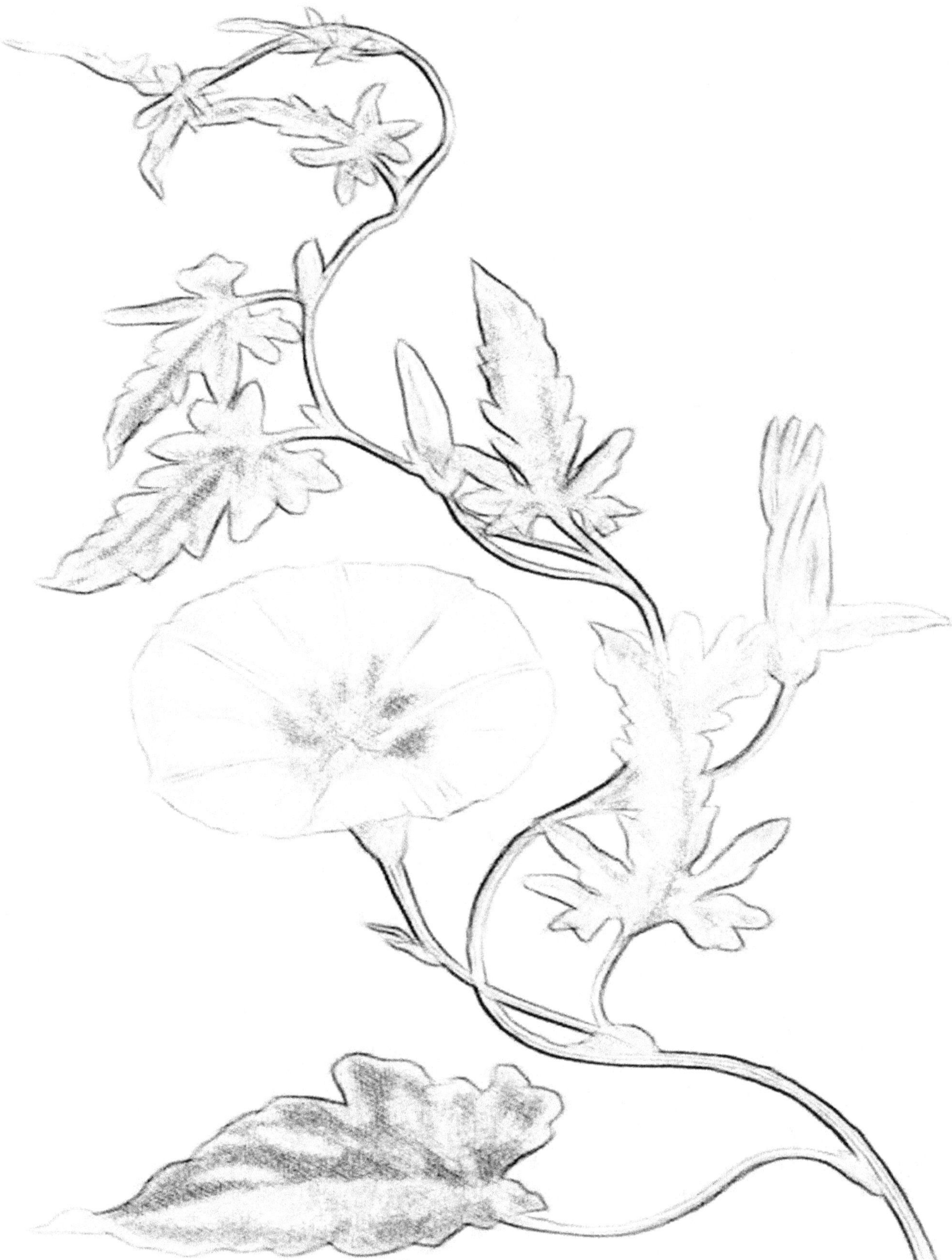

www.ingramcontent.com/pod-product-compliance
Lightning Source LLC
Chambersburg PA
CBHW081622170526
45166CB00009B/3066
9781519738011